UNDER
THE
FIG TREE

UNDER THE FIG TREE

Stories of Prayer-filled Moments

William Breault, S.J.

Ave Maria Press, Notre Dame, Indiana

For one who knows how to listen
and wait, Clarence Miller.

Acknowledgments:

I would like to thank Jeanie Templeman, a friend who took an interest
in this book, read the manuscript, made some suggestions, and typed
the final copy.

I would also like to acknowledge the help and support of Mr. and Mrs.
Robert Greer, a generous, outgoing, and deeply Christian, couple.

International Standard Book Number: 0-87793-198-4 (hardcover)
                                    0-87793-199-2 (paperback)

Library of Congress Catalog Card Number: 79-56689

Photography: John David Arms, 30; William Breault, S.J., 38;
        Joya Hairs, 6; Rising Hope, 66; Freda
        Leinwand, 58; Theo Robert, 12, 18, 50;
        Joan Sauro, C.S.J., 92; Rick Smolan, 95;
        Justin A. Soleta, 80; Chick Woodfall, 44.

Printed and bound in the United States of America.

AN UNLIKELY TABLE OF CONTENTS

I. PRAYER IS SEEING AND BEING SEEN

Nathanael and the Indian Guru

Under the fig tree may seem like a strange title for a book on prayer. The title itself comes from an incident mentioned in John's Gospel — the first meeting between Christ and Nathanael. You may remember it. Andrew, after being called by Peter, his brother, to meet Jesus, tells a friend, Nathanael, that he has met the Messiah, from Nazareth. Somewhat cynically, Nathanael replies, "Nazareth? Can any good come from Nazareth?" Andrew answers by saying, "Come and see." Somewhat reluctantly, Nathanael meets Christ, who (typically) sees through his defenses and tells him that he is a man without deception or guile. Surprised that Jesus could see into him, Nathanael blurts out, "How do you know me?" The point is, that in his meeting with Jesus, Nathanael felt revealed, opened, or known. Christ's answer to Nathanael is the title of this book: "I saw you *Under the Fig Tree.*"

When this incident from scripture was being explained to me, years ago, as a novice just entering religious life, there was an indirect suggestion that Nathanael was up to no good under that fig tree! And this was the reason he was so surprised by what Christ said. In other words, he was *seen* under the fig tree doing

7

something suspect, perhaps flirting, or worse! And yet, he could have been doing something *good* under the fig tree. Perhaps he was praying, seeing and being seen. After all, a good place to pray is under a tree.

I remember a striking example of this years ago in Honolulu. An Indian Guru was speaking to a large audience of Western people. He had the reputation of being a holy man who could show others the path to take to calmness and peace in the midst of a hectic life. He opened his talk with a story showing the difference between the way of the East and that of the West.

Western man, he told his audience, is a traveler on a journey. His journey carries him through life and beyond. And he discovers while on his journey that the main obstacle to peace and happiness is the self, symbolized by the shadow he casts under the glaring light of the sun. It is, after all, the self that keeps getting in his way; so Western man, in an effort to escape the self, his shadow, walks faster — but so does the self! If he can escape the self, he will be at peace, so he walks even faster. Still the shadow follows. Then he starts to run to get away from this "thing" that is ruining his life. But it makes no difference: No matter how fast he runs, the shadow keeps pace. Finally he falls to the road, exhausted by the effort.

Along that same road came a stranger from the East. He saw the crumpled man and took pity on him. He reached down, touched him, and asked him what was the matter. And he soon found out, as the wounded man explained how he had come to the realization that his self was dominating his life. He told about his compulsive attempts to rid himself of the evil influence, ending in failure, exhaustion and despair.

The stranger suggested to the broken man that he come with him and sit beneath a giant tree whose branches broke the rays of the sun. It was peaceful beneath the giant tree; and once both men were seated, resting against the trunk, the stranger from the East asked the man from the West, "Where, now, is this self, the one you were fleeing?" The restored man looked for his shadow, but of course, the shadow was no longer visible in the shade of the tree.

The conclusion the Indian Guru stressed was that people from the West should sit under a tree more often. Perhaps Nathanael was doing just that, sitting under a tree, praying, seeing and reflectively considering life.

The Lord Jesus, we are told, *saw* the deepest truth of all, about struggling and suffering in life, about death and the acceptance of his father's will, and the promise of victory over evil, beneath a grove of olive trees — a different kind of seeing, perhaps, troubled and filled with pain, yet true sight and deep prayer.

> Down the hill
> Beneath the olives
> I stood
> And eyed the slanted shadows
> That barred the praying place.
> The darkness
> Was transparent,
> Filled with the colors
> Of music
> Dropping silently
> Into pools of water:
> Ever-widening circles,
> Hollowing out a space
> To wonder in.
> Below,
> The lights from a thousand cities
> Of a lost world
> Flickered
> In expectation

That poem — if it can be called that — came right after praying, under a grove of olive trees. I had always wondered what it would be like; so one night with a full moon above me, I walked down a steep hill to an olive orchard and prayed.

Nathanael could have been praying under the fig tree when the Lord saw him!

I would like to suggest as a tentative, general definition of prayer that it is a *seeing*, a looking for or at someone — and getting looked at, or seen, too! The story told about the Cure D'Ars, which may be apocryphal for all I know, fits well here. He reportedly asked an old peasant who spent long hours in the church praying, "What do you do as you sit there hour after hour?" The peasant looked up, shrugged, and said: "Well, I look at Him; and He looks back at me." Prayer is seeing and being seen. And I think that most of us sense this. Of course, there are different kinds of seeing and being seen. To be seen by another (really seen), is to be revealed — delivered over to that person — and this is even before words are spoken! That's why many people fear going to a psychiatrist, or a priest, because they are afraid of being seen. They fear the knowledge the other person will have because of being able to see into them. For to see is to have knowledge. But what these people are really afraid of is that someone else will see what they already suspect is true and have never closely looked at.

If love is present, however, we don't mind being delivered over, so to speak, into the hands of someone who sees us. In fact, it seems like we go out of our way to reveal ourselves to those we love just so they *can* see into us. Jesus sees others in just this way — with love; and Nathanael knew it, as did Peter and the other disciples. He sees others in a way that delivers them over to him, and that experience moves them deeply. That is, I believe, what happened to Nathanael, and also to the Samaritan woman mentioned in John's Gospel. After a conversation with Jesus, which got too close for comfort, she ran into the nearby town shouting: "Come and *see* the man who told me everything I have done" (Jn 4:29).

The one seeing her is the one who hovered over the chaos and darkness on the first day of creation and drew out of it light (to see by), life, beauty, and goodness — and that One *saw* that it was good!

What is prayer? It's seeing and being seen. Yet it's more than that, too. Years ago, any worthwhile book on prayer would have a neat four-or fivefold division of prayer into the prayer of praise, prayer of petition, and so on, and certainly prayer does praise, and ask; but somehow prayer itself eludes neat divisions that satisfy the mind and not the heart. Tell me that prayer is to see and be seen — I understand that. Do you remember how Peter, despite his promise to remain faithful to his Lord in his passion, betrayed Jesus? Yet he was converted and wept when the Lord, tied and mishandled — the one he loved so much — turned and without a word looked at him after he had solemnly sworn that he didn't even know who this Jesus was. Peter was *seen* at that moment, and his heart was delivered over to the Lord and healed. Sooner or later, all our neat words and phrases go dead, and we are left only with the heart that is wounded, as it was with Peter. Then it is that the Spirit moves within and teaches us to remember, to pray without words.

All prayer really begins with the heart. And the heart must be seen — and somehow know it — before it can see.

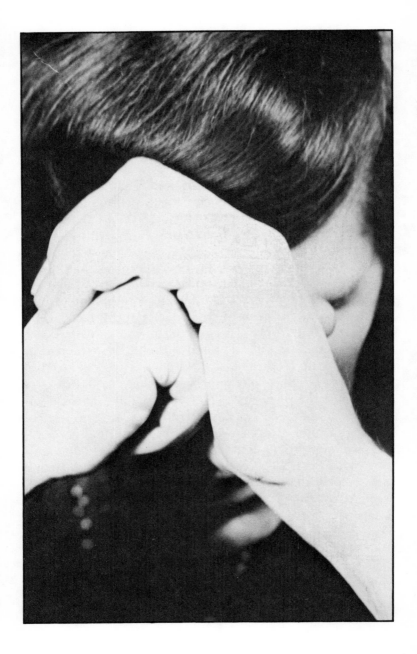

II. NOT BEING AFRAID TO REVEAL YOURSELF

Jeremiah and His Struggle with God

There is a quality or an attitude in prayer that for lack of a better way to describe it, is called transparency. When a man is transparent in prayer (willing to ask God about anything and everything in his life, direct and to the point), he is in danger of discovering himself, and in that discovery there is a knowledge of God. You can't be truthful without at the same time coming to know God. They go hand in hand, for God is Truth. When a man is honestly seeing God, he gradually becomes "transparent" — he can share all of his life, even his negative emotions of disgust and fear — and, strange as it may sound, even protest against God!

I remember once talking to a rabbi about the meaning of life and suffering and prayer. The rabbi, a brilliant man, said: "We Jews have one thing you Christians don't — the sense, in prayer, of a protest to God about the way things are going." What he said seems true enough to me. Many Christians would rather suppress negative emotions in prayer — as though both our personal interior world and the exterior world we live in were all sweetness and light. Somehow they think it is wrong to be frank and honest in prayer; all of their prayers must sound like they were written by an English scholar for use in a crowded cathedral on Sunday! We are often not honest with God because secretly we fear to discover our own selves — perhaps our own anger. We fear "transparency." So we run the risk of not discovering our true selves and the Lord present within.

Jeremiah, a prophet who lived about 600 B.C., loved God. He followed the Father's call and went about proclaiming his word to an unwilling audience. He was not only a prophet, but a man of prayer as well. And in his prayer, Jeremiah complains bitterly to God of the cost he has to pay to proclaim his word, which far from being treated as any kind of good news, was rejected — along with Jeremiah! His vocation to be a prophet made him lose friends, caused him to become the laughing-stock — the butt of jokes and the center of intrigue on his life. And Jeremiah, a sensitive person, felt this deeply, but he didn't suppress it in prayer. He didn't bury it beneath a pile of pious garbage and memorized phrases when he prayed to God. He spoke from the heart — a true cry from the heart — when he shouted out to God:

> You have seduced me, Yahweh, and
> I have let myself be seduced; You have
> overpowered me; You were the stronger.
> (Jer 20:7)

(Notice the imagery! "Seduced"! "Overpowered"! God must like a fight — so must Jeremiah. It's just that Jeremiah lost the fight!)

> I am a daily laughingstock, every-
> body's butt . . . The word of Yahweh has
> meant for me insult, derision, all
> day long. I used to say (notice this!): "I will
> not think about him, I will not speak in his
> name anymore."
> (Jer 20:8-9)

Now that is what I call *transparency* in prayer. That man is not afraid to tell the Lord exactly where he is. Complaint? Yes. Disgust? Yes. Anger? Yes, that too. And that is what he discovered about himself. God can do a lot with a man who is transparent in prayer, since the man is not hiding anything. He is bringing it into the light, and God is the light. There is no healing for something that lays buried in the darkness by intent.

In another section of Jeremiah's writings, he says of himself and his lot in life which was caused by the Lord's call:

> My heart is broken within me,
> I tremble in all my bones
> I am like a drunken man,
> A man overcome with wine —
> Because of Yahweh
> and his holy words . . . .

(Jer 23:9)

It's clear in the mind of Jeremiah where the trouble comes from: God and his word. And he takes his protest to God. Talk about graphic language! Listen to the following prayer, and this is not hyperbole. Remember also that when Jeremiah wrote the following lines, the Jews did not have a belief in the afterlife, at least in any way that would seem to make it a better place to go to than this present life:

> A curse on the day when I was born,
> No blessing on the day my mother bore me!
> A curse on the man who brought my father the news,
>
> "A son, a boy has been born to you!"
> Making him overjoyed.
> May this man be like the towns
> That Yahweh overthrew without mercy;
> . . . since he did not kill me in the womb . . .
> Why did I ever come out of the womb

> To live in toil and sorrow
> And to end my days in shame!
>
> (Jer 20:14-18)

Strong and powerful words from a man filled with anguish, but willing to face the anguish and protest against God because of it.

In another prayer which most Christians would think pure blasphemy, Jeremiah, after telling God how he loved his word when he was younger and felt joy of heart before he had to proclaim the unpleasant prophecies to Israel, says:

> Do you mean to be for me a deceptive stream
> with inconstant waters?
>
> (Jer 15:18)

Remember, Jeremiah is talking to *God* in prayer! And he says of him that he has become a polluted stream, and a polluted stream kills life! Inconstant waters no man can trust. Jeremiah is hurting, but he still prays as Jesus Christ did when strung up on the tree of the cross, abandoned by his own people, disciples, and seemingly, God:

> Lord! Lord!
> Why have you forsaken me?

Whose side are you on, after all?

After repeatedly saying that he would no longer think of God, no longer preach his word, even try to forget him, Jeremiah complains:

> I used to say, "I will not think about him,
> I will not speak in his name anymore."
> Then there seemed to be a fire burning in my heart,
> Imprisoned in my bones.
> The effort to restrain it wearied me,
> I could not bear it.
>
> (Jer 20:9)

Jeremiah tried to blot the memory and the word of God out of his heart, but the word became like a fire urging him to speak. Another graphic image — the *fire* of God's word that burns in a man's heart! This is the same fire that the two disciples on the road to Emmaus, after Christ's resurrection, felt. They, too, were discouraged, depressed, wanting to throw the whole thing over. They met a stranger who spoke to them words of scripture, and their spirits picked up. Later that same night, as they returned to tell others of their experience (for the stranger was Christ himself), they said:

"Did not our hearts burn within us as he talked to us on the road and explained the scriptures to us?"

(Lk 24:32)

In the case of Jeremiah, the fire of God's word won out. That fire is the cause of great tension in a man's life and prayer.

III. USING YOUR EARS TO LISTEN

Duke, the Nine-Year-Old Theologian

Prayer is not just being seen and seeing, not just becoming transparent; it is also listening. Listening is a great art, and an art must be worked at, or it dies out. How especially true this is for a professional listener! Yet there is no class of people that is exempt from listening. Real listening is prayer.

People vaguely suspect that real listening *is* prayer, since it is an ability to receive. Many times I have visited convalescent homes and seen people who had been important at one time, well-known and loved — lawyers, doctors, priests, judges. In their past, others were spellbound by their words or actions; juries were swayed, congregations inspired, but there is no evidence of that now. They lie on their hospital beds, staring upward at the ceiling, their mouths half open, and — listening! Yes, listening. Finally, we do listen, it seems, for sounds from another world — sounds that perhaps we who are in the midst of life can't always hear.

Still there are many moments of listening before the final listening — moments of joy and happiness, of tender love in which the only proper response is to be quiet and listen. There are moments in everyone's life when a hush comes over him, like the quiet moment after a brilliant piece of music has been played—that quiet moment just before the thunderous applause.

Some prayer is like that, a listening that can be caused by a letter we receive, or the fog rising out of the river and blurring the trees, giving what was monotonously dull a touch of mystery. Something that someone says, perhaps just a chance remark, but one which fills our need, can make us listen. We enter into ourselves, to listen within, as is so often said of Mary in the Gospels. She pondered the events that happened to her, and which she did not always understand. There are great silences, especially in Luke's Gospel, connected with the Virgin Mary. One must listen between the lines, so to speak, in order to catch the inner working of Mary's heart and prayer.

The problem with listening effectively revolves around the fact that we too often hear what we want to hear, instead of what the other person is saying or feeling. With this approach to listening, of course, you can never be wrong, I suppose. That is one kind of certitude. And perhaps the desire for certitude is what causes us to listen for what we have already decided we are going to hear.

Along with this ego-centered kind of listening goes a too facile way of judging people for what they are, even before they are known! No mistakes are made that way.

I remember one night, a few years back when I became acutely aware that I had been listening with only half an ear, at best, to what people were saying—and most of the time, too. That night I realized I had badly misjudged a young boy, nine years old. I had him all figured out as a hyperactive, tough city kid with little or nothing inside his head except street sports, fighting, and the desire to do what he wanted when he wanted. Yet, I also saw fear in his eyes—a child's fear of a world that has lost meaning for him — the adult world. Yet, the obnoxious quality of his hyperactivity prevented me from really knowing him; nor did I take much time to get beyond that facade. I was sitting in the parlor of his home reading a newspaper. Strangely enough, what I was reading (as I looked back later on) seemed to prepare me for what was to come. God speaks to us in ways that we hardly expect. He was speaking to me in the following quotation from an article written by Louis Cassels, the writer who for so long popularized religion in syndicated columns all over the United States. Here is what I was reading as the hyperactive boy was making a nuisance of himself nearby:

> If a parent is lucky, his inquiring child will demand to know, at some point, "Where is God?" That's a door-opening question. It enables the parent to say that God is everywhere, like sunlight. But you are most likely to encounter his presence in your own heart where he makes himself known as the spirit of love.
>
> (From *God's Image*, Los Angeles *Herald Examiner*, Saturday, August 15, 1970)

The above paragraph was part of a longer article which I found well worth reading. I finished reading and started to leave the house to pick up a friend coming in at the San Francisco International Airport. I rarely write in a diary, but what happened on the way to and from the airport so impressed me that I stayed up late into the night to get my thoughts down on paper. They were that important. Here is what I wrote that night:

"I had planned a few days' rest intending to go to San Francisco, but one thing after another came up to destroy the rest I had hoped for. Yet, as so often happens, something I had not expected also happened to make it al worthwhile — a talk with a nine-year-old boy!

"The boy is hyperactive, fear-filled, still aggressive in fighting his fear — also, fatherless. I really hadn't intended talking with him this evening, but I had to go to the airport to pick up a friend and wanted company. I invited his sister to go along with me. Then, about to leave the house, my conscience suggested that Andrew, the nine-year-old, would feel left out if I didn't at least invite him to go along. Surprisingly (I thought), the boy wanted to go with me. His sister, so eager to go on the trip down the peninsula with me, got into the back seat of the car and fell asleep immediately. Her brother was in the front with me. I was stuck with a hyperactive kid!

"As we drove along, the boy started to ask me questions. The first one was: 'Does God have a beard?' I thought about this for a while and replied: 'Well, no . . . but maybe his Son does.' That seemed to satisfy him, but he wasn't through with the subject of religion. A little while later he asked what heaven was and where it was. I told him that heaven was all around us but we couldn't see it. He thought for a bit, then said: 'Heaven could be anywhere then, couldn't it? Even in a hole?' I thought that over cautiously but didn't come up with a satisfactory answer, so I said: 'Well, Duke (his nickname), it's like walking into the end of a rainbow.'

"We were silent for a moment or two, then he asked me if I knew that Peter had a brother named Andrew. I said that I did know that, and he asked me how I knew about it. I told him that I read the same book that he did. Then I began to tell him about Peter — figuring I was on good ground, safe. (Since I had known the boy, I had never seen him in such a mood.) I described the time the Lord was teaching people down by the lake and the crowds became too big to handle, so he asked Peter to take him out in the boat. After teaching from the boat, the Lord told Peter to let down his nets for a catch of fish, and when the nets almost broke, 'What,' I asked him, 'do you think Peter was thinking?' Duke answered, 'How did he know that the fish were there? That's probably what he was thinking.' When I said that Peter told the Lord to 'Get away from me because I am no good!', Duke said that Peter was afraid because he thought Jesus was just a man at first.

"By now I was deep in this conversation, forgetting that I was talking with a child and feeling like I was on 'holy ground.' I, myself, was learning by what I was hearing, and I should say privileged to hear. Also, by now, Duke was on a different aspect of God's presence. This time he asked if I could see God, or rather, if anyone could see God. I said, 'No . . . but he's like the wind. No one could see the wind either,' I explained, 'nor did they know where it was coming from. They didn't know where it was going, couldn't taste it, see it, feel it, but they knew it was present.' I felt pretty good about my explanation. Duke answered back after a pause. 'But I *can* taste it when it comes in from the sea, and I can feel it when it tears at my clothes, and I can hear it when it makes noise and moves the trees.'

"After that, I figured that I had better forget my theology. I was being beaten on my own ground, so I said: 'Well, that's right, and that's the way that God talks to us. Sometimes he talks to us like the wind going through the pines, sometimes like the wind blowing through the birches. Each one is different.'

"Duke thought some more and said: 'I feel that God talks to me, but I can't understand his words. Sometimes he says: 'Don't do that,' or 'Do that.' As I listened, I thought to myself: 'Well this kid is keyed up already. He probably has a super conscience that's talking to him.' I was going to correct him because I thought that he was already too fearful. So I said, 'Yes, but that could be you talking to you and worrying too much, like you did yesterday about serving your first Mass.' 'No,' he said, 'That's *my* voice, not God's.' I decided not to make any more comments.

"We were both silent for some time, then out of the blue came this remark: 'I know why you can't see God.' Since I was losing at this game, I decided to learn why *he* couldn't see God. So I said, 'Okay, why can't you see God?' After all, I didn't bring this subject up in the first place; he did. Duke came back with: 'Because he would be solid, wouldn't he?' I was on the verge of correcting him when some inner urge suggested that I shut up. I began to think about what he had said. It sounded better and better the more I thought about it. He saw quite well why we couldn't see God. If we could *see* him, it would mean that he would be a material object. 'Okay,' I thought to myself, 'I'll listen.' My ideas about this boy were radically changing.

"On the way back from the airport, and after we had picked up our guest — and after I had warned him, too, to keep quiet and listen because Andrew was doing the talking tonight — Andrew said: 'You know, I would like to be someone else, like a baseball player, but I'm no good at it.' I thought of trying to show him that we are good at being ourselves, so I remarked: (expecting a quite different answer from the one I got) 'Well, Duke, what do you think I'm good at?' Quick as a shot came the answer. 'You're good at talking to people (he had been doing most of the talking), telling stories, at listening, and at hexing people in games!' I laughed at that, and all three of us were silent. His sister was still asleep in the back seat of the car.

"We were driving through the park and getting closer to his home when Andrew, still in a pensive mood, said: 'You know, sometimes I go into my room and I close the door. I sit down and I grow quiet. Then the big noises become small, and the small noises become big, and I always feel rested and better after.' Very carefully and quietly I asked him what were the big noises that become small. 'Oh, sounds like a pot or a pan falling to the floor.' I didn't dare ask him what the small sounds were.

"Just before we arrived at the curbing in front of his house, which was on a hill, Andrew said: 'I felt like I wanted to tell these things to someone, but couldn't; but now I did and I feel much better because I got it out.' Then I told Andrew, 'Well, thanks, Duke, I got to know you more in the past hour than I had in the past four years because we talked — really talked.' He asked me what I meant, and the only way I could think to explain what I had said was the image he had used already. So I said: 'We listened for the small sounds people make, not for the big ones that cover them over.' He was silent.

"This evening (these are still the notes I took that night) was one of those rare moments in time, when age and time mean nothing, when this boy was transparent and communication as perfect as this life could allow. I felt like I was walking on holy ground, causing growth by carefully listening to his world, in his way, with his symbols — a great privilege. A great, grace-filled moment of growth for me and for him; for me in understanding how profoundly little ones experience the same things I do, humbling to be able to listen and grow because of it. He taught me more of prayer than many a priest has!

"How to listen! Could we listen, we would be stunned into awe and joy!" (End of diary)

Prayer is listening. No theologian in the world can tell me that Andrew and I were not deeply involved in one long moment of prayer that evening. It isn't as though there were just the two of us — rather, it's as though the two of us were caught up into the presence of another, and in that presence, we understood; we came to know the inside world of the other, where in the words of Louis Cassels, ". . . He makes Himself known as the spirit of love."

Weeks later, still dissecting my experience with Duke, I wrote the following lines — but not before much more listening.

To the Lord of the Wind

As they walked
    by the Sea,
    the small boy asked:

"Can you see God?"
And the priest hesitated,
    struggling
    to frame the answer.

"Well, . . . the wind blows,
    and . . . you don't know
    where it comes from — nor where it's going,
    do you?

"No," the boy replied.
"You can't smell it, either, can you —
    yet you know it's there,
    don't you?"

The hurdle passed,
    the priest inhaled deeply,
The wind he had described,
Confident
He had defended well
    God's honor
    to the mind of this nine-year-old
    mystic.

"Yes, I *can* smell the wind,
    when it comes from the sea.
And I can feel it, too;
    and taste its salt."

The priest paused.
So did the boy.
Each caught in the mystery
    swirling about them.

After a time
    the boy spoke:
"I know why you can't see God."

The priest waited—
    the same age, now,
    as the boy
    teaching him—

"If you could see God,
    he would be Solid,
    wouldn't he?"

They walked on,
    the two of them—
An unlikely pair
    on the edge of the sea.

The surf laced the sand
    beneath their feet;
And off at a distance,
    the great breakers
    crashed
A hollow, cracking sound.

Like the sand,
Absorbing water
    beneath his feet,
The priest's mind
    was filled with the moment.

The boy spoke again:
"Sometimes I go into my room
    and shut the door.
Then everything grows quiet.
The big sounds
    become small,
And the small sounds
    become big.
I sit there,
    and wait—

> And I always feel better
>   after."

> The wind picked up some of the froth
>   from the sea
>   carrying it high,
>   up on the beach;
> And the waves washed
>   away
>   the footprints
>   molded in the sand.

Prayer is listening, and we need to listen especially today. Why? For a very simple and often unobserved reason. We have become glutted with so many sources of information seeking entry into our hearts, that we can no longer hear our heart, nor the heart of nature — least of all, the heart of God. In Christ's time, a man could perhaps become exhausted with too many people making demands, but today we not only have a greater number of people making demands, often trivial, upon us; we also have machines that feed us a steady supply of information, and also make demands upon us, so much so that it's as though a layer or wall has grown up between us and what is most real. The noise of so many machines — telephones, record players, stereos, television sets, tape recorders, computers, duplicators of every sort — so fills our minds and hearts that there is no longer any room to just be quiet and hear what others are saying, or the world, or our own inner selves.

How can we expect to hear God if this is our daily diet? As someone said: "To come into the presence of God, a man must come home to himself." But our selves are occupied with too many technological demons! There is no room to come home!

There is another reason why silence is difficult, and, therefore, listening. To be able to really listen, you have to let go of yourself.

To really listen takes a high degree of detachment from your own self, not in a negative way either.

A sponge lets the whole ocean pass through it. It's always full. To listen, you have to give yourself away to what you're listening to. Listening and surrendering, or as they used to call it, abandonment, are not really all that different in meaning.

In our language we have a word that means "entirely taken up with something," *enthralled.* To be enthralled means to have surrendered your very self to, say, a brilliant piece of music being performed. The *thrall*, from which the word comes, was a slave. The first and original meaning of enthrall was to be made a slave to someone, to be given over to that person. To really listen is to give yourself over to what you are listening to. In the case of prayer, it is to give yourself over to his presence, to listen in the great empty wastes, to reach beyond the realm of words and images, waiting for the sound of God himself, which is silence.

IV. WAITING IN PRAYER

The Lady from Honolulu

The prayer of waiting: perhaps this is the prayer we do most, when nothing seems to be happening within ourselves or outside ourselves either. To wait is to develop patience. Paul, that fiery, impatient apostle, puts it neatly when he says in his letter to the Romans: "And we also rejoice in our troubles because we know that trouble produces endurance (patience), endurance brings God's approval, and His approval creates hope" (Rom 5:3-4). It may well be that endurance comes from waiting in prayer and leads to hope and God's approval. Still, despite the inspired word, people who are seriously interested in discovering God find waiting a most painful experience. I have heard many good Christians who were "right" with God tell me they could no longer pray as they used to. When they try, their only experience is one of abandonment in the sense of being a derelict at sea!

I remember speaking one day with a lady who was right with God and experiencing just such a waiting period. She wanted to pray but couldn't. Her prayer itself had become a dark pain. From that conversation, these lines came:

Honolulu

Palms swayed
And grace-filled people
Hurried past
To deadlines,
While we sat
Illumined
By the soft blue glow
Of fired glass.
Below the presses moaned
In anticipation;
And we talked
Of the spirit
Falling
On its prey,
Stealing a man's pride,
'Til in pain
And humility
Gentleness was born.
She said, "You've changed!
Your arrogance
No longer shows."
I nodded
Tracing lines of heartbreak
In and around her eyes —
A response, I wondered,
To an unguarded "Yes?"
Probably not.

"I can no longer pray,"
She wept,
"Nothing but darkness
Comes to mind,
And absence."

And I recalled a desert island
One crisp morning
Half a life ago —

Walking a beach
Beside a turquoise sea,
Watching the sun come up
Alone;
And sensed deep within
The loneliness
Of that moment.

It is little consolation to tell such a person that the great mystic, John of the Cross, says that one of the characteristic signs of progress in faith is darkness and the sense that nothing is "going on." But that kind of message sounds like answering a riddle with a riddle. When someone is patiently waiting in darkness, it matters little that someone else can define it and locate it on the ladder of prayer. Darkness and dryness are feelingless states. And *that* is the problem! Feeling seems to have been lost. What once provoked joy and the ability to endure in God's love no longer moves him. He is feeling-less, and feeling *that* state keenly. It seems to the person in such a state that God doesn't care, or if he does, he's concealing it. Little by little, the thought overtakes him that God is displeased with him. Then guilty feelings arise which become an endless circle leading nowhere but into more dryness and darkness. At this point, prayer becomes not just darkness, but agony as well. At this point, too, all former images of prayer, God and self break down. This is part of the problem. And this is what God is bringing about, but it does little good to tell someone that.

Perhaps the *only* way to understand and accept this kind of waiting is to forget all the explanations and go back to nature, observing it, listening for it. The need at this point is not for rational schemes or explanations, but for experience.

Perhaps a clue to why we wait — and must do so — can be seen in nature. There, we see the necessity of land lying fallow neither planted nor worked, after having produced abundant crops. If the land could feel, it might just feel dead at this point, as though it were useless. Human nature seems to be similar in that respect. It can take just so much. Then it falls back upon itself, exhausted. In a sense, it is burnt out and must remain still and seemingly unproductive in order to silently and painfully regroup its vital forces.

It is precisely the working of God at a profound level within the soul that causes the darkness! And that's why we must be patient at times and wait. It's as though what was going on is so profound that reason doesn't have a part in it. It's beyond reason — deeper. God is working directly with the soul on an experiential level. The light is so bright that preconceived ideas of God, his presence, the value of others — are being profoundly altered, burned away, you might say. In this kind of state, reason, our normal way of controlling and grasping life, making it manageable, is like a small poverty-stricken waif, out on the street, hearing the noise of a party within the house but unable to enter, since the doors are shut tight. The example limps — since the person of prayer who is in the darkness waiting doesn't think there is a party going on anywhere, least of all within!

Another example from experience that might be helpful in trying to understand the value of waiting is what takes place in the life of a creative person — one who works at art. It's an attested fact that creative people can stay in gear just so long. Then comes the crash, depression, or whatever name you wish to give it. On the face of it, this state seems to be useless. Yet down below the level of consciousness, profound changes are taking place. The old images have been burned away, expressed. In the resulting vacuum, new life — psychic and spiritual — begins to sink its roots.

As I said earlier, none of this makes much sense, nor gives much consolation to a person in darkness, waiting. There is no way to get out of waiting, except to wait, especially where growth and life are concerned. Perhaps in the long run, the only useful thing to do when the darkness is upon you, or life seems dry — and all this is reflected in your prayer — is to sit under a tree, or on a riverbank, dangling your legs in the water, watching the circles of water form. But wait you must.

Still, there will come a time when the waiting will bring fruit — then it all will have been worthwhile. Waiting always involves time. We wait for what is up ahead in fear or desire — but almost always in ignorance, for the simple reason that we can't read the future. What many people don't realize, even people who pray — though perhaps they do sense it — is that there are two different kinds of time. And when you're waiting, it's good to know that fact. One kind of time we set our clocks by. It's called chronological time, from the Greek word *chronos*. Our world, it sometimes seems, runs by chronological time. This kind of time is linear. When a man asks you how old you are, the answer — unless you are a comedian or a saint — will always be in terms of linear time: "How old are you?" The thirty-year-old man answers, "Thirty years old." He might be only twelve years old as far as maturity goes, and that brings up the other kind of time that we wait for, kairological time, from the Greek word *kairos*.

Kairos time is the time of the child in the mother's womb. The child will not be born exactly nine months after conception. It will be born usually when it is time for it to be born. An event is being prepared; when it is ready, according to the laws of its own inner development, the child will be born. The same is true of love, vocation, beauty, death. Although a man can tell you when he will be forty-five years old, he cannot tell you when he will fall in love and get married. There are two kinds of time.

The artist is always dealing with the second kind of time, kairos time. He must wait for kairos time. It will disclose itself. The creative muse will not be taken and made to conform to the time that we run our world by. It is not an eight-to-five kind of thing. It has its own laws, just as the baby in the womb. It's abornin', but it will not be born, productive, until the moment is ready. Paul says in Galatians: "But when the fullness of time came (kairos), God sent His Son, born of a woman . . . ." In other words, God didn't wait for the clock to get around to a certain year before he sent his Son.

Prayer is always dealing with kairos time, and you can't rush kairos time. You can't speed it up. That would be like planting a seed, waiting a day for growth, seeing none, and then stamping your foot on the seed shouting out, "Grow! Dammit, grow!" The seed has its own laws, inner laws. So does prayer, especially waiting in prayer.

When Andrew and I talked together intimately that night, the time was ready — not chronological time, but kairos time. He was ready. I was ready. The situation was there; the need and desires all came together. It was kairos time, God's time, not man's.

So much unhappiness in life comes from trying to speed up kairos time. It's like trying to squeeze out a vision. It can't be done. The only way to get through waiting is to wait. But it does help to know that something *is* going on. There will be a kairos time for you. It's not just an endless string of events tied together with little or no meaning. When the time is ready, God will reveal himself. Meanwhile, the only thing to do is be faithful — and remember! For memory has a role in bringing God's help to us.

Remember the times in the past when God spoke to you clearly. Remember when you were touched by his grace and your life changed. Remember sharing that grace and enthusiasm with others, never counting the cost — remember. Even pray about remembering. This, after all, was what the prophets thundered at the chosen people. *Remember!* Remember the goodness of God toward you.

Why? Why should they remember? Since they had begun to forget! The sin is in the forgetting. And there are times in life when the only way we can manage to get through is to hold on by *The Skin of Our Teeth*, as the great playwright Thornton Wilder put it. We do so, often, by recalling moments of grace in the past, as the Hebrews recalled the deliverance from Egypt.

"Do this in remembrance of me," the Lord Jesus said the night of his betrayal. Memory has a definite and essential role in bringing God's grace and love to us. It has, likewise, a role in prayer, in recalling that love. "I will send you a helper," Jesus promised, "who will cause you to remember."

What do you do while waiting, feeling like a derelict ship on an unfriendly ocean? Realize something *is* going on. Kairos time will come. And, remember.

V. PRAYING WITH A PENCIL

The Sixteen-Year-Old Girl

A few years back, I was speaking with a friend of mine, a high school girl, and we touched on the subject of prayer. The girl was intense, shy and quite intelligent. I asked her: "Do you ever pray to God other than vocal prayer?" I guess I was expecting her to say that she was into contemplation! She said, "Oh, yes!" with the look of someone caught doing something good but embarrassing. She looked down at her hands on her lap, then half sideways at me, and said, "Only I don't exactly pray to God; I write him a letter, but I never address him, except in the third person singular. I go into my room and write there. I guess you could call it a kind of prayer."

I was so surprised at her answer that I almost laughed. She saw the beginning of the smile and reddened with more embarrassment, which caused me to cut short the smile and think more deeply about the fact that this was privileged information from deep within. She was revealing something very private about her inner life.

That sobered me. So I said to myself: "Well, that's nice — formal, but nice." The next thought was, "Who am I to say how someone should pray?" We talked some more, then dropped the subject. Six or eight months later, I became very dry in prayer. Although I felt that I was trying to pray and to do God's will, and even though I prepared my prayer carefully, when it actually came time to pray, to enter into God's presence, I felt as though I had no thoughts or feelings. I couldn't move beyond the point of apathy! Then my friend's seemingly strange practice and our conversation came to my mind. Why not write a letter to God and tell him just where I was at? Still, it seemed like a stupid thing to do. As though one needed to make a mark on a sheet of paper to draw closer to God or to become aware of his presence; as though God had to get a letter, or receive a religious poem before one could pray! Fortunately, I didn't listen to my own objections. I began to write about how I felt; that I couldn't feel anything. I wrote that I found it hard to forgive and that I found the beauty of his world too sharp at times. More often than not, as I continued the writing, I would put down the pencil after ten minutes or so — I was ready to pray, wordlessly, to God, or just to sit in his presence.

The effort to put down my thoughts on paper revealed them to me. But it also revealed the working of God within me — as this book does!

I prayed this way for three years and wrote three books doing it, though that was not my intention. These are books of prayers about God's presence, my weakness, and the beauty of love and friends, his hidden grace, and the uneasy fear of death — all of the things that a man would be expected to pray about.

The reader can understand, now, where the following prayer-poem came from, what kind of experience produced it.

A Prayer of Desire

How true it is, Lord,
That I pray better,
Sometimes,
With a pen in my hand.

It's as though
I must see something
Flow out from my being
   toward you;
For it's too great a burden
To pray the wordless prayer
In your presence.
   I must formulate
   My feelings
   And read them over,
   For they clarify my affection
   For you—
   And many times
   Recall it!

How often
I read what I write
And I'm humbled
by what I read,
As though it came from a third party
Deeply in Love
And searching for you:
   The way I want to be!
But my feelings have become dulled
By habit
And the subtle anxiety
Of depending upon myself.

What comes out of our pen, if we are truthful, may shock us. It certainly did me. One particular morning, feeling dull and apathetic, yet strangely aware of God's presence, I started to talk to him, telling him where I was, and how I felt. I wrote it down on paper, and later changed a few of the words, polishing it up. But the basic prayer conveys what I felt and clarified it to me, helping me to sit content in his presence.

O Lord,
I want to talk to you
To say something—
But I don't know what to say!
I feel your presence
　　close to me;
And yet at the same time I also feel
　　your difference
　　from all that I know:
One invites—
The other inspires awe
　　and humbles my eagerness.
You are so strange
And different,
　　Like some wild thing
　　Held in captivity,
　　Easily wounded
　　And shy—
　　　Yet holding the hunter captive!
Embracing and giving life
To all who seek
　　to embrace You.

By the way, when God "moves in on us," so to speak—well, there is no preparation for this kind of prayer. It's *his* time, and his movement automatically focuses our hearts. When God touches us, of his own accord, and in his time, there is no effort on our part. Nor can we ever produce such a thing. It's a gift. Someone has said, and I believe it, that God doesn't necessarily reveal himself to a man at prayer, but always to a man *of* prayer. When such a thing happens, all of our efforts—which we must make—are bypassed. We can take no credit for it. Once again we must recognize kairos time, God's time. And he alone, without any previous warning or any external cause, can enter the depths of a man's heart. Paul met his time and his God on the road to Damascus. He didn't pick the time nor did he pick God either! It was, instead, Christ who chose him and revealed himself to him. In one instant, the work and effort of years were redirected as Paul, in a flash of light that blinded him, became a Christian.

Ever after, he spoke of Christ Jesus appearing to him, calling him to be an apostle. Yet he says of the vision only that it was light, a light that redirected the course of his life. This was God's time, and no effort on Paul's part produced that moment — that meeting on the road when he realized that the dead, crucified Galilean was alive and present to him in the very people he was torturing and putting to death. That experience of God shaped his life and his entire theology, too. In all of his writings, he refers back to the moment in his life when he met Christ. The meeting became a center and wellspring of action — a focal point for all his prodigious energies and reasoning. There is no preparation for such a thing as this.

VI. PRAYING WITH GOD'S FIRST GRACE:

The People Who Were Oblivious

Prayer is to be seen, and to *see*, sense, hear and feel everything, too! But especially nature. The Fathers of the church and the early theologians spoke of creation as God's first grace, his first gift — that is, the medium in which we are graced, in and through which we discover God. It almost seems today as if man has forgotten nature itself! Our contact with Mother Nature is often so indirect that we become dulled in the way we perceive her. Milk no longer comes from cows, but from cartons. The poet, Gerard Manley Hopkins, said it long ago: "Nor can foot feel, being shod." We see images of nature, TV shows about it, records of its sounds. The real thing, however, is at a distance. So, too, is the grace that comes from contact with it. Nature speaks of God if we approach it with respect.

Recently I gave a retreat, and I think that many of the people making the retreat wanted to pray. They were surrounded by beauty, and God's first grace — creation — high on a hill overlooking mountains, lakes, and paths in and around the trees. I am sure that many of the retreatants thought of prayer *not* as seeing and responding to what beauty there was, but as making sentences in their heads. Yet what is the purpose of such beauty? Why would God create such beauty unless he wanted us to sense and appreciate it, and in doing so learn something about him?

During a break, I walked outside to be quiet and look, listen, and breathe. I was struck by the fact that very few of those making the retreat were doing the same. I wondered if they had forgotten how! And what a sight there was to see: deer tracks, horse and dog tracks in the fresh morning air, small flies in a squadron suspended in light between giant redwoods in perfect flying formation, balanced and touching wings, the scratching of dry leaves in the underbrush as quail nervously protected their young. What a feast for the eyes and the ears! And what an insight into God's beauty and truth. Man is the only animal that can realize and see that beauty, the only one who can put it all together in an act of wonder and praise. Man is the summit of creation, the one who gives it a voice before God.

To walk quietly through such a place, listening, looking and reflecting on what has been heard and seen, is prayer — prayer that leads to God just as surely (in fact, more certainly) than making sentences in your head. Too often when we make sentences in our heads we are talking to ourselves, and often for our own benefit, too. Perhaps we are afraid of silence. Yet, in silence, if we listened for the voice of God and the infinite variety of ways in which he speaks to us, we would be far from bored or distracted.

Perhaps what I just said sounds strange. But recall the temptations Christ underwent in the desert. Do you remember how he repulsed the devil when he suggested that a miracle would cure his hunger? "Man," the Lord said, "does not live by bread alone but by every word that comes forth from the mouth of God." And on the first page of Scripture, in the Old Testament, God spoke a word and the universe came into existence — a word for the seas, sun, moon, the land, trees, vegetation, birds, and finally man — all are his words; that's the point! We are nourished by his words, by *every* word coming from God, just as surely as we are nourished by bread. To apprehend these words we must *see* them, hear them, not just read them, but actually apprehend them through the senses.

One day I was reading a section from the Book of Sirach, which was included in the breviary, the book of psalms, prayers and lessons that for centuries has constituted the prayer of the church. The words suddenly came alive as I got past the print aspect and sensed the meaning: We are nourished by his words, all of his words — and this is no small mystery! Try reading slowly and thoughtfully the following poem, written thousands of years ago:

> He sprinkles the snow like fluttering birds;
>> it comes to settle like swarms of locusts.
> Its shining whiteness blinds the eyes,
>> the mind is baffled by its steady fall.
> He scatters frost like so much salt;
>> it shines like blossoms on the thornbush.
> Cold northern blasts he sends
>> that turn the ponds to lumps of ice.
> His is the plan that calms the deep,
>> and plants the islands in the sea.
> Those who go down to the sea tell part of its story,
>> and when we hear them we are thunderstruck;
> In it are his creatures, stupendous, amazing,
>> all kinds of life, and the monsters of the deep.
> For him each messenger succeeds,
>> and at his bidding, accomplishes his will.

The point is that all things speak to us of God, but meditate carefully on the rest of the section I was reading:

> More than this we need not add;
>   let the last word be, he is all in all!
> Let us praise him the more, since we cannot fathom
>   him, for greater is he than all his works;
> Awful indeed is the Lord's majesty,
>   and wonderful is his power.
> Lift up your voices to glorify the Lord,
>   though he is still beyond your power to praise;
> Extol him with renewed strength,
>   and weary not, though you cannot reach the end:
> For who can see him and describe him?
>   or who can praise him as he is?
> Beyond these, many things lie hid;
>   only a few of his works have we seen.
> It is the Lord who has made all things,
>   and to those who fear him he gives wisdom.
>
> (Sir 43:18-35)

A man wrote the above lines; for only a man can give a voice to creation. He alone can put it all together in an act of wonder and praise, in prayer. But he must first sense these things, be aware of them, see them. He must be nourished by all the words spoken by God.

There are too many books on prayer that are filled with abstractions. I wonder if the author got his knowledge of prayer originally through the senses, then forgot all about them.

There are no tree leaves without roots, and the root of prayer is our experience of our world, of God, and one another. In one way or another this knowledge comes through the senses. The senses shouldn't be left out of prayer. It dries up if they are. Saint James says in Scripture: "How can you say you love the God you can't see when you don't love the brother you can see?" What he is saying is that the visual, the visible, is favored over the in-visible in touching God and in being touched by God! Too easily we can make of religion and prayer something abstract, dried out — something in our heads alone.

That will never happen if the senses — the experience of our world, our eyes and ears, and hearts — are part of our prayer, as they certainly were for Christ, who describes his father's kingdom in terms that a child and an artist can easily understand and grasp. And why? Because that is the way he saw. He must have reflected a great deal on nature, on growth, on the habits of animals, on the seasons and weather, in order to speak the parables that still have a hold on man's memory and imagination. No one could spend a night on a mountaintop without a rich experience of what was going on around him, and through that experience, be led more deeply into trusting in the darkness and silence.

VII. ACHIEVING A SENSE OF PROPORTION

The Temporarily Paranoid Monk

Concentration has become a bad word. To be able to fix our minds on one thing only seems to connote mental gymnastics, a brain-busting withdrawal from the realm of life and sensation, an exclusion of all distractions *by force*. In my opinion, this is a very limited notion of concentration. I would rather say that to concentrate is to be concentric — to circle around something with your whole attention — not just your mind, but your whole person. People concentrate in this way when they are interested in what they are doing, whatever it is. It is *not* a forced thing, contrary to popular belief. The man who habitually can't concentrate is missing much of the beauty and joy of life. The kind of concentration that hurts our heads usually comes from fear or desire, especially the fear of not getting what we desire!

The person who stands enthralled before a work of art (which by the way, he does not own) — that man is concentrated. Real concentration brings with it a sense of wholeness, peace and integrity. It is the opposite of being at your wit's end, driven in so many different directions that you no longer know who you are or where you are going. In fact, that is what *distraction* is! Distraction, the word itself, comes from the Latin and means, "to be pulled apart in different directions"; literally, to be dragged apart. And who, in today's society, hasn't had that experience?

There are moments of prayer that are pure concentration, and usually they are short, but not always. These moments leave us with a feeling of being integrated, at rest, or all together. And there are things that we can do sometimes to prepare ourselves to enter into God's presence in this way. They might be called focusing agents, like music, for instance, which for some people acts like the focusing lens of a camera, drawing their scattered consciousness and energies together in a moment of silent concentration, the prelude to prayer. Writing a letter to God or a walk in silence can lead some people to the quiet moment in which they are no longer distracted. Reading something from Scripture or some other worthwhile source can gather and focus our attention; the same with poetry and song. The trick is to know when to rest *in the quiet moment!* So often I have found myself reading, beginning to wonder, approaching the moment of prayer. Then, instead of putting down the book and remaining quiet, I kept right on reading, and the moment passed. That is gluttony. And often enough I have spent time I have put aside for prayer just reading when I was being called to silently muse, wonder, or savor what I had already read.

Sometimes it is enough to read one line of Scripture and sense that you are already filled. To go one step further, at that point, is to lose the moment — gluttony again! Quantity, rather than quality! In a moment of doubt, for instance, a person can come across this line from Scripture:

> This is what the Lord asks of you,
> Only this,
> To act justly,
> To love tenderly,
> And to walk humbly with your God.
>
> (Mi 6:8)

He is struck by the message and how well it applies to him. Then, thinking to get more by reading more, he leaves behind the message intended for him — the one that spoke to him — and ends up worse off than when he began. It takes real sensitivity to your own needs to stop when (in the expression of the gold miners) you hit "pay dirt." Dig your treasure there. Forget the possible treasure troves of the future. The person of prayer or the person who wants to learn to pray must live for the *now*, not the future. And prayer, by the way, makes it easier to enter into the *now* — no small thing today when the emphasis is on programming the year two thousand even before we know that we're going to have a year two thousand!

We are so used to the idea of structuring the future in order to control it that we have almost forgotten we have a present.

To be able to fully live in the present moment, focused, is quite an accomplishment, one worth praying about and for! An Oriental teacher of religious thought spoke of living in the present moment as being centered, "all there" (or here!) with all of your energies. To meet a person who is centered is to meet one who is together — focused — fully engaged in whatever it is that he is doing. Prayer makes it easier for a person to be centered, even inclines him toward being centered in the *now*, but not in a hedonistic way, not trying to squeeze every last bit of pleasure out of "this moment" as though there might not be another moment like it. That's not what it means to be centered for a man of prayer. Rather, he is fully engaged in this moment, but this moment has a history. It had a beginning and will have an end. This moment, this *now*, is in the hands of God, as all moments are. That knowledge gives man some distance. He is not being swallowed up by the moment.

The man who prays knows that there is a beginning and an end to life. He also knows, or soon learns, that there is a veil beyond which he cannot perceive God's existence and the web of grace woven into our personal relationships, but he can and does sense this through prayer.

Real prayer delivers us from the tyranny of the present moment and allows us to center or focus ourselves more fully. The fact is that the tragedy we encounter, the death or reversal, the intense pleasure or peace of the moment we are in, is not *all* of life. Such knowledge, which comes from prayer, can deliver us from despair by placing our experiences against the larger format of life itself. Once this happens, we can see the event in perspective. Too often, we can be deluded by the present moment, magnifying it all out of proportion.

When this happens, a good day or a good experience means that the whole of life is and will be good forever, just like the moment; or a bad experience means the whole of life will be bad forever, just like the present moment. These are delusions that lead to false hope and despair. To prove their falseness, just reflect back on some experience that you have had that not only seemed painful at the time but stupid and meaningless, and which proved in time to be just the opposite. What looked evil somehow worked itself into something good. It is God who rescues us, converting the evil that happens into good by drawing good from it.

In and through prayer we are able gradually *to see* our lives and then our history touched by goodness and evil. We grow in the knowledge that we are called beyond immediate upsets and successes, even though it is *in* and *through* the experience of these things that we are called. In other words, we become detached through prayer which allows us to see our lives in perspective. This is a gigantic step. For to see our lives in perspective, it's necessary to get the right kind of distance. That's what detachment means! Prayer allows us to get that distance. It's the old story of the man (who didn't pray) who couldn't see the forest because the trees were in the way. Prayer allows us to back off and get a little better view — by which, notice, we can see *better*; therefore, more deeply enter into what we see.

Once upon a time — that's the way all good stories used to begin for children — a monk was walking down a country road. It was early in the morning, and he was going to meet some good friends who lived a great distance away. (This was hundreds of years ago, of course.) He had on his brown robe, his head was tonsured, and his sandals were slapping against the road raising little clouds of dust in the sun. Around noontime he began to tire. He was also hungry. It was time to eat; only he had forgotten to bring a lunch, so he began to get edgy, even a bit paranoid about the length of the road, the heat of the sun, and the "why" of the journey. He was completely uncentered or distracted around 1:30 p.m. when he stumbled upon a rock right in the middle of the road. He hadn't even seen it, so taken up was he with his own thoughts and concerns. With the pain of the wounded toe, however, he immediately became aware of his surroundings. (Pain has a way of centering us quickly. That's why it's related to prayer.)

What was that rock doing there? His mind started off in a new direction. Why would a rock be right in the center of the road *he* was walking on? As though someone had intended it? (The rock started to grow in size.) That's it! Someone had put the rock there, just so he would stumble on it! (The rock grew even larger.) Someone who didn't like him — (the rock by now had grown so large that it blocked the road entirely) — his mind raced with the names of people who didn't like him and perhaps wanted to get even with him.

By this time, the rock had become an insurmountable mountain. The monk was defeated, totally distracted. He sat by the side of the road in the shade of a tree, staring up at the gigantic mountain that had risen up to block his efforts and frustrate his plans.

Along that same road came a lady, and seeing the distracted monk, she went over to him and asked what was the matter. He told her the whole story of his desires and good intentions, how he had been wounded and blocked by the great mountain someone had put in his way. The lady spent some time with the monk talking with him. Then she went over to the center of the road, picked up the rock and threw it to the side. To say the least, the monk was surprised! He was amazed at this feat of strength. Ever so slowly the reason why he had started on his journey in the first place came back to his mind — yes! The journey to see his friends! *That* was the important thing. After sitting awhile longer, collecting his thoughts, he got up and continued his journey. As he left the place of his accident and his fortunate encounter with Lady Prayer, he noticed that the mountain was only a rock after all, hardly big enough to prevent him from making his journey and seeing his friends.

Prayer gives us distance and perspective if we are faithful to it.

VIII. PRAYER CHANGES YOUR EYESIGHT

Two Killers

What happens to a person who prays consistently? His eyesight changes. That is one of the most significant effects of prayer. How many times do you see a cold-blooded murder, reported in a newspaper, one committed without any reason that is obvious, just a senseless action? Two men, for instance, enter an apartment and terrorize three old people huddled together for mutual support. The men take what money they can extort from the old people, then because one old woman doesn't have enough to give them, she gets clubbed on the head with a soft drink bottle. The two men gag her, and while she suffocates, they open up the refrigerator, sit at her breakfast table, and eat and drink in full view of their dying victim and her terrified companions.

Imagine for one second what kind of eyesight these killers have, how they look at the world around them — at old people, for instance; how they look at children; police.

Life itself has little or no value to them. They must see it as a hostile, chaotic series of unrelated happenings, with victory going to the cunning, the strong and powerful. It's obvious that they don't pray! Otherwise they would *see* differently. Had they prayed, they could not have killed the old lady. Unfortunately, this story is true.

Prayer changes the way we look at things, the way we see ourselves and our world. From a hostile, aggressive and chaotic series of unrelated events, gradually there emerges, for the praying person, signs of a web that ties together people and things that happen. The world looks like a different place when one has perceived that all men have a common Father and are, therefore, related to one another. It isn't as though evil ceases to be, but through prayer, one's eyesight is changed so much that he begins to see others as related to himself. He is no longer an isolated shred of humanity forced into a shell of loneliness. Prayer reveals a man's heart to himself, and in that revelation he sees the hearts of all men and of God.

Prayer makes us related to our surroundings, to our fellow men, above all to God, the cause of all relationships.

That is the kind of eyesight that will eventually change the world from being a place of evil to one of goodness. The transformation must first take place within the heart, and that is the realm of prayer. Prayer teaches us to see differently, and the changed vision is what changes life. It's curious that we generally accept this in other branches of knowledge and experience and run from it when considering prayer. In art, for instance, in order to teach people how to draw, it is first necessary to teach them to see differently. There are all kinds of experiences to achieve this change of eyesight, such as looking at the model and not at the paper while drawing. The drawings that result from such an exercise look strange at first, but with practice and experience the beginner's eyesight is so changed that he is no longer a beginner. He has a grasp of form, value and line that he never could have gained had he not changed his perception, his eyesight.

This is the case with prayer. It teaches us to see differently. It changes our eyesight with practice and experience.

Arnold Toynbee, the great English historian, was reported to have said that all the great men of history had one practice in common: periodic retirement during the day, week or month to a place of prayer or meditation, a place where they could bring their minds and hearts together in a moment of concentration, a moment that brings about vision — seeing differently, as God himself sees.

Seeing — or learning to see — involves what artists call positive and negative space. There is such a thing as negative space in art, the space that is not painted — the white space — unused. On this page that you are reading, it would be all the space that is unprinted, all the space, then, between the letters and lines, and the space on the borders of the page. That is the negative space. The print is positive space.

In order to read, to see, there must be both positive and negative space. Without that contrast between negative and positive space, there would be no such thing as reading or writing. Try to imagine for a second a page with only negative space. All white! Obviously, there would be nothing to read. Or try to imagine all positive space, i.e., all print. Without the white or negative space, the paper would be all black! Once again, there would be nothing to read. To be able to read or write, paint or draw, there must be both positive and negative space. And so it is in prayer. There is and must be positive space when we are conscious of prayer, God, affection, good thoughts and so on. But there must also be negative space.

When prayer is largely composed of negative space, you wait, peacefully. And that is an art, just as surely as painting a picture.

There can be both positive and negative moments within the same prayer, a thought, a half-expressed desire and, then, perhaps nothing. Waste time during those moments—they are necessary for vision. Don't be too eager to fill them with forced thoughts and verbal or vocal prayers. Do nothing in an interesting, quiet way.

What do you do when you're doing nothing? Watch things grow. As a Buddhist master of novices told one of his subjects: "Watch the rocks grow." Or better, listen to the sound they make while they grow! Stare at the shadows; rejoice in color, *tasting* it. (Have you ever wondered what a color tasted like?) Sense life, in other words, and through life you will be led to a deeper prayer. Nature, beauty, color and life don't lead away from God, but *to* him.

In every real prayer there must be both positive and negative space. To know that is to be delivered from the fear that "I'm doing nothing." The answer to that is: "Yes, that's right. God is doing it, but not in a way that you can pat yourself on the back for, congratulating your goodness." But certainly in a way that will make you a deeper person, more in love with God and life. And your eyesight will change.

I remember one day in particular when I experienced both positive and negative space in prayer, a dull day in a crowded city, next to a river. As far as I was concerned there was nothing going on inside me and not much outside either. I was a stranger in the house where I was staying. At least, I felt that way, and my prayer reflected the way I felt—blank. Then I met a friend I hadn't seen in years. How that changed my eyesight! Later I reflected on how I passed from a negative space mood to a positive. The point is that both are necessary, as I think you'll see in the following prayer-poem, which flowed from the experience I had — an experience of prayer in the widest sense.

O Lord God
Thank you!
For life
   with all its bewildering intensity
   and color —
It really is people, Lord
   who help me to see.
Without the challenge
   of their personalities;
Without their love
   and concern,
   the color fades from my life —
But today, of all days
A monotonous day
   filled with grayness
   and little expectation
   of newness or life —
Today I talked with a friend,
   given to me
   by you;
And we discussed shared experiences
   and sorrows
   of long ago.
Our hearts grew warm
   with recollection
   and interest —
And then, as I walked
   by the river,
   later, alone —
And caught the night reflections,
Green, silver, and red,
Projected on the water
   by the lighted city
   at a distance,
I was filled with love for you
   and for the gift of life

Feeling it, in all its *newness*
  deep within me.
A light rain falling
  reminded me
  of where "up" is;
And each gasp of breath
  was sharp
  and cold,
A pleasure to my lungs —
And then, Lord, the knifelike sharpness
  of life itself —
This transient
  brilliantly colored
  flux of things
  before my eyes —
Life!
So precious
  and spendthrift?
Shone out
  fraught with promise
  and mystery —
For this
Lord of the wild things;
Lord of the whisper
  and the wind,
I thank you.

IX. WHAT'S YOUR GOD REALLY LIKE?

The Psychiatrist and the Runaway Son

You can't pray and stay depressed. That may sound like a pretty strong statement, but look at it this way: If you stay depressed, you'll stop praying. If you keep on praying, then you'll have to "have at" the cause of the depression, and that means facing the things and people you have not forgiven—the ones you still hold resentments against. Prayer is an immediate gauge of what is going on deeper down than the mask we usually show the world.

If you are consistent in trying to pray, then you must come to terms with yourself and the hurts that you harbor: the ones you have been saving, getting ready to cash in at the right moment.

One of the first effects of depression on a person is the feeling that "God doesn't like me." Another is the feeling that "I must have done something wrong." And a third is the inability to pray. Why pray, after all, to a God who doesn't like you? That's why I said that you can't stay depressed and pray. One or the other will drop. If you continue to pray, then your prayer will lead you to

seek guidance or direction, and that will ordinarily lead
to a solution for the depression, provided you have a
desire to forgive.

If you continue to stay depressed (feeling that God
doesn't like you, etc.), you'll drop prayer. The man who
is honest enough to shout out his anger to God, at least
knows the cause of his anger — or soon will find out!

I remember once hearing a psychiatrist speaking
before a spellbound audience. He was a Christian. He
began his talk by saying that 90% of the people who
come to him are depressed and want to be cured of their
depression. What they don't know, however, is that
anger (in most cases) *causes* depression, and according to
this man, people, while wanting to be cured of their
depression, do not want to give up their anger. Why not?
They are angry at some*one*, and that someone will not
change; so they remain angry at him. The function of
anger is to make the other person change. When he does,
the depressed person will give up his anger. Of course the
other person could be dead — which makes it impossible
for him to change — and the depressed person still must
deal with his anger if he is to improve.

The depressed person doesn't see the connection between his depression and his anger. Part of therapy is getting him to see that connection, and then, finally, identify the person or persons with whom he is angry. But
even at that point, the psychiatrist can't get the person to
give up his anger. He can only point it out; help him to
identify it; to face it.

There is only one way of giving up anger at someone,
and that is to forgive him for what he has done. No
psychiatrist can get a patient to do that.

Talk about forgiving, and once again you enter the
realm of prayer.

Stored-up resentments, hatred that is buried and

suppressed, anger and a desire for revenge — all these things will "out" in prayer. It is just a matter of time (kairos time). When they do, the experience of prayer often becomes distasteful. Once they are recognized, however, and owned up to, they become the material for prayer itself. If they are not owned up to, prayer will eventually cease.

How much stored up anger! It's a wonder we can get off an Our Father once in a while with all the resentments we save and nourish.

People wonder why they can't pray or don't even want to. Perhaps it is because there is so much unfinished business. To see with the eyes of Christ, we must grapple with our lack of forgiveness and with the wounds that we introduce into the world, into our own families! Not to do so is to cut yourself off from your own self.

However, it is good to reflect that it's impossible to pray long, or be relaxed, in the presence of a God who is a judge only. This is another aspect of the way that prayer changes our eyesight. Imagine yourself a prisoner caught in a crime. You must appear before the judge, and he has the power to electrocute you for your crime. Well, you certainly might pray when you're in his presence — a prayer motivated by sheer terror! But that is not Christian prayer. Even though it's true that there are moments of terror and fear in every man's life, still Christian prayer does not grovel on the ground before an all-seeing eye that can condemn to the electric chair. At best, such an act before such a judge is a distortion of prayer and God. It is more a creation of man's fear than a discovery of the true nature of God! Imagine for one moment trying to be your real self in the presence of such a God. You can't make any mistakes (or you're done with!).

The image of God as judge only distorts the whole gospel message. It makes prayer impossible and cancels out what Jesus Christ came to show and tell us. Man can only reject such a distortion. And yet, I remember reading some years ago in a religion book that God the Father wanted, above all, justice, and the only way to achieve that justice was to take the life of the most perfect man on earth, Jesus Christ. His life, given in a crucifixion, would make up for the infinite offense that man had created by his sin. With the crucifixion of Christ, justice would be fulfilled; God would be avenged. In other words, he retaliated.

Imagine loving such a God? The author of the book that I was reading went one step further (so great was *his* passion for justice). He said that Mary, his mother, that most perfect of women, was standing next to the cross, and she so wanted the Father's will done (i.e., justice), that even though it wrenched her heart to see the nails being driven through the hands of her son — had the Roman soldiers stopped crucifying him, she would have picked up the hammer and nails and finished the job herself, even though it tore her heart out. Some mother! And what a ghastly distortion of God! That's the God as judge only, who wants justice at all costs. Thanks be to God and his Son, Jesus Christ, that the book I was reading was *not* part of the revelation of Jesus Christ about the real nature of God, our Father.

When Jesus describes at length what his Father's attitude is toward us here and now, he paints a picture — artist that he is — a picture to store in the mind and heart and never forget. It's that picture dwelt upon and acted on that changes our eyesight. The main point of the parable of the prodigal son is to show what the Father is like. Then we can understand what reconciliation and conversion really mean.

The picture that the Lord paints is that of a father who had two sons. Everyone is familiar enough with this parable, but all too often in explaining it, reconciliation is stressed and the One to whom we are reconciled is passed over too rapidly. As an aid in suggesting some thoughts about the parable related to prayer, I'd like to recall the story which appears in Luke's Gospel, Chapter 15:11-32.

The father owned a fine farm, good acreage, cattle, crops. At the time of his death, the farm would have been divided and given to the two sons, not before. The younger of the sons came to him one day and demanded his share of his inheritance, right now! And the father gives him his share. It seems foolish to us, reading these lines. Why would the father do such a thing? He knows the boy is going to spend it foolishly. It even seems that the father is giving the boy the means to get further away from him. The father in the story is Christ's picture of what his Father is like. We are the sons.

The father gives the boy the money to leave home. It breaks his heart but no words are said like, "Why don't you stay around awhile and grow up instead of making a fool of yourself?" The father doesn't act that way. He doesn't want the boy to leave him, but he respects freedom too much to coerce him. He hopes, however. What good would it be after all to have him remain home against his will? Love is that way. It desires freedom, not slavery. And infinite love created freedom for that purpose, a return of love. So, even risking rejection, the father gives him the money he needs to leave him, which he does, going off to a strange glittering city filled with promises (for those who can pay) but short on fulfillment, as the boy soon finds out. Remember that the son thought that he knew what would make him happy *apart* from the father. His father knew on the other hand that he couldn't achieve that happiness apart from him. That's what makes his silence so powerful.

In the son's mind, his happiness depends upon

money and what it can buy. After the money ran out, along with his friends, dejection and despair set in. He had lost his position of dignity as the son, in a way, since he was now doing a laborer's job feeding the pigs. And if the father in this parable spoken by Christ is a picture of God, well, where was God now that the son was down and out sitting in pig swill and despair? — In the boy's *memory!* That's how close God is to us. Notice what happened. The boy started to think about the laborers on his father's farm — how well treated they were. His memory was recalling how good his father really was. Then, and only then, came the clear realization that he had sinned. And that's when he woke up. He saw clearly that he had sinned against God and his father. The sin was in forgetting. The healing came when he remembered. He wanted to be happy, and his happiness was tied up with his father. He learned that much. Now, if only he would take him back.

What would *you* have done if this son of yours who had taken his share of the inheritance came back home asking to be accepted? Would you, justly, rebuke him? Something like: "Ahh! I told you so, didn't I? See what you get when you don't pay attention to your father? You don't deserve to be one of the family, throwing your money away. Money I worked hard for!"

But that's not the way with the father, who saw the boy a long distance down the road before the boy saw him. He had been waiting for this moment, hoping for it, going out each day and looking down the road saying to himself: "My son will come back." Christ's words describe the scene far better:

> While he was still a long way off, his father saw him and was moved to pity. He ran to the boy, clasped him in his arms and kissed him tenderly.
>
> (Lk 15:20)

And he had just spent half of the father's bank account!

I doubt if I would have met the boy with an embrace and kissed him!

And listen to what follows:

> Quick! Bring out the best robe and put it on him. Put a ring on his finger and sandals on his feet. Bring the calf we have been fattening and kill it. We are going to have a feast, a celebration. . . .
>
> (Lk 15:22-23)

That boy is going to get it all back! The whole inheritance! Incredible! No wonder the other son who had been faithfully working the farm was mad. He's the one who would get depressed. Who wouldn't? That's only human, and the point of the parable is that God's love, our Father's love, is far superior to human love — greater, kinder, more understanding. Compare the love of both of the sons for their father with the love of the father for his sons in this parable to see just which one comes off superior. As a matter of fact, neither one of the sons seems to have had much real love for the father. One was a prodigal, a superficial spendthrift, and lazy on top of that. The other was so angry that his father accepted the prodigal back into the family that he wouldn't come into the house to talk to him. The one who stayed home and worked was a miser, a puritanical self-righteous prig. The kind that burns witches. His father (God!) had to come out to plead with him not to be angry that he loved his son enough to accept him back.

The father's love for both his sons is the strongest thing about this parable. It is one hundred percent pure, not selfish — not condemnatory. The father accepts anger, ridicule, disbelief. His sons talk down to him. They take his money, eat his food, hate each other. Still the father loves them both and unconditionally, too. He accepts both of them *as they are*, defects and all — as God does us.

That is the kind of love we need so badly. We can be healed by that kind of love. And love is the opposite of depression. Depression says, "I am of no value." Love says, "You are of infinite value." Keep in mind that Christ is telling us what our Father is like. You can breathe in the presence of this God, relax with him, be seen by him and not shrivel up and die, nor fear being electrocuted. The sons were caught in crimes. They came before the judge, and the judge embraced them, kissed them, pleaded with them, and finally, held a feast to celebrate the fact that they decided to remain with him. That's our Father, the one Jesus Christ revealed to us, the one we pray to.

John, in his gospel, has one line that stands out like a beacon on a dark overcast night:

> No one has ever seen God;
> It is the only Son,
> Who is nearest to the Father's heart,
> Who has made him known.
>
> (Jn 1:18 JB)

How many people reading the Gospel knew that the father had a heart? And a heart *for* us? That is the truth the Son came to reveal. In the light of that truth, the parable of the prodigal son is one of the most important parables in the New Testament. If you want to see clearly what God is like, what kind of judge he is, then go back to this parable and look carefully at the father. His picture there is not distorted by time, nor spiritual writers with an axe to grind. No theologian needs to explain it. It is obvious from one reading that the Father loves us, and it's easy to enter into his presence with all our faults and sins and relax there. It takes a long time to get this through our heads, because at one time or another, we are like the prodigal son or his older brother. Both had a misconception of what their father was really like.

For the prodigal son, the moment of truth came, figuratively, while sitting under a fig tree. At least he had enforced leisure from his endless round of burning himself out with pleasure. He found leisure, the leisure to pray and turn back to his father, in the pigpen! And notice how the Spirit of God moved the boy — in and through his memory. He went from depression to hope to love. God is in the unconscious as well as the conscious mind; and Jesus Christ said that he would send us the Spirit, who would help us to remember. In this parable, we see a clear example of God's Spirit moving someone to conversion, to return.

It's interesting to watch the reactions of high school students to this parable of God's mercy and love. They have such a strong sense of justice — one which says in a subtle and often overlooked way that love is earned — that they most often identify with the son who remained at home, the son who never disobeyed, and who was justifiably angry with his father. Certainly most high school boys would not give the prodigal a party, to say nothing about giving his inheritance back. Yet in their hearts, they want the father to do just what he did — accept his son back completely because they can envision themselves doing the same thing the prodigal did, squandering everything. It's their sense of justice, fair play, of earning something that prevents them from seeing that God's love comes before anything we do, not as a result of something that we have done.

The Father's love for his prodigal son didn't decrease because the son made a fool of himself, nor, by the way, did it decrease because his older son wanted to go on a witch-hunt as soon as the younger boy returned. No, he

loved both of his boys, unconditionally. Their good or
evil actions didn't cause the father's love to suddenly appear or disappear. In other words, their actions weren't
the cause of their father's love. They themselves were the
objects of that love. It's this insight that is at the heart of
Christian prayer. Listen once again to Scripture,
remembering that love and forgiveness are what drive
depression and self-hatred out!

> If you love only the people who love you,
> Why should you receive a blessing?
> Even sinners love those who love them!
>
> And if you do good only to those who do good
>   to you,
> Why should you receive a blessing?
> Even sinners do that!
> And if you lend only to those
> From whom you hope to get it back,
> Why should you receive a blessing?
> Even sinners lend to sinners,
> To get back the same amount!
>
> No!
> Love your enemies,
> And do good to them;
> Lend and expect nothing back.
> You will have a great reward,
> And you will be sons of the most high God.
> For He is good to the ungrateful and the
>   wicked.
> Be merciful, just as your Father is merciful.
>
> (Lk 6:32-35 *Good News for Modern Man*)

The point of the above Scripture passage is to *be like*
your father. The son who stayed home and worked while
his younger brother ate up the family inheritance could
not *be like* his father. He thought that his younger
brother forfeited the father's love and his respect. In
other words, he felt he had a right to be hostile and ag-

gressive toward him and the father as well since he was so blind that he couldn't see. That is how *the just* often sin, through blindness. Everything is justice for them. They don't see that in reality everything is a gift.

It is in prayer that we begin to see that it's all a gift. The prodigal began to see that in the pigpen with a moment of prayer (kairos time) in which he remembered the goodness of his father. Jesus says:

> But I tell you who hear me:
> Love your enemies,
> Do good
> To those who hate you,
> Bless those who curse you,
> And pray for those who mistreat you.
> If anyone hits you on one cheek,
> Let him hit the other one, too;
> If someone takes your coat,
> Let him have your shirt as well.
>
> (Lk 6:27-29 *Good News for Modern Man*)

It's grating on the nerves to read something like the above Scripture passage. It seems inhuman. Like the older brother, our sense of justice is violated. To really read and understand something of what Jesus is talking about in this passage is to be on the road to holiness.

Why be kind to the person who hates you? Why bless those who curse you? And if someone hits me on one cheek, I'm not about to offer him the other one. He's got something coming all right, but it's not the other cheek! And if someone cuts in front of you in a crowded street when you have worked all day and are tired, when you're trying to get home and take a good hot bath, have a drink, and be with the family, give him the whole lane? Not at all! Instead, I'll reach up under the dashboard for the instant destruct button, and destroy him right on the spot! God may love him — well, he can have him!

The older brother was so angry
That he would not go into the house;
So his father came out
And begged him to come in.
"Look," he answered back to his father,
"All these years I have worked like a slave for
   you,
And I never disobeyed your orders.
What have you given me . . . ? "

(Lk 15:28-29 *Good News for Modern Man*)

The point is that the older son thought he had a right to persecute his brother and his father. He himself was innocent.

Why be kind to the person who hates you? Why bless those who persecute you (which, of course, you can't do without the Spirit of God within you)? Because this is what God is like and if you wish to belong to him, you must make room for the way he intends to live within you. He loves those who are unkind to him, who curse him, who wish him evil. He does not repay evil for evil. He loves even the older brother who in his anger would like to turn the younger son back to the pigs.

If you are going to pray for long to the God of Scripture, then the word Father will begin to take on a new meaning, and your actions in life will begin to resemble those of the father in the parable of the prodigal son. For some of us, it might take a lifetime. But if we are faithful, the Spirit of God's love will shape our lives through prayer, so that we begin to grow into something resembling his Son, who was motivated by the opposite of resentment and depression — love and forgiveness!

X. SUFFERING AND PRAYER

The Naked Oak and the Blind Leper

There is a place in prayer for suffering. But there is a catch here that good people don't reflect upon too often. Suffering is darkness. It causes darkness. That's why it hurts. That's why it can also isolate us. Usually we associate prayer with light, not darkness. I remember hearing a fine priest complain once that he couldn't pray while in the hospital. He was in there for major surgery, and it was a serious operation. After the surgery, he tried to pray but couldn't. I understand how he felt but, looked at from the outside, his desire was all too painfully obvious. He wanted to pray. Why couldn't he? He was suffering. He was in the darkness. He *was* praying, the prayer of suffering.

How do you pray the prayer of suffering? You just suffer. And here is what you suffer — the darkness.

To suffer means to bear, to carry. When a person is suffering, it often means he is walking in darkness. To pray in such a state merely means "to suffer the darkness." To let it be; to be helpless and know that it is all right to be helpless. God's eyes shall see where yours are closed — nor will they be closed forever.

One day I got a phone call, asking if I would visit a woman I had met and talked with, but didn't know well. In the weeks that followed, I got to know her!

She had just been told, after testing and surgery, that she had cancer and had no more than a few months to live. The news didn't shake her; in fact, it seemed to make her faith stronger. She had, in a way, been waiting for this moment; and, although she was happily married with a fine family, her deepest love — which embraced her family — was for God. It sounds trite to write these lines. What is convincing is the example of this woman, accepting in faith the greatest of suffering — the loss of her husband and family — while still maintaining peace and joy and a profound spirit of prayer that affected all who came to see her. Words about that experience are, at best, secondhand.

She decided to die at home. Her mother, sisters, husband and children cared for her — but she was the one who consoled them! And that much I witnessed. She helped those who visited her to come to grips with their own unresolved feelings of death. She saw what she was doing as her mission in life at this time, one she succeeded in, judging from the number of people who came to see her.

A few days before she died, I visited her. She could no longer rise from her bed. At one time she had been a beautiful woman. Now she resembled a skeleton, barely covered with flesh — but her spirit was strong. She endured her suffering.

I sat down beside her and said something or other, I don't remember what, and she turned to me: "Father, the pain I feel now is unlike any pain I have ever felt. It's no longer mine. It seems to be the pain of those who are suffering all over the world."

The pain of Christ!

Right after she died, I visited her and in a prayer-filled moment, laid my hands upon her head, praying God to accept her, knowing in my heart that he did. She lay stiff and white, all marks of beauty gone, her lower jaw tied to her head with a handkerchief; and I contrasted in my mind the grace, beauty and strength she once had with this sticklike figure.

Later that day, I sat and pondered her death, how I had got to know her, and the meaning of her life. I was looking out a window. It was a gray day, overcast and still, like a death had happened in nature itself. A great oak stood, leaves gone, stark. The following prayer-poem took weeks to live and hours to formulate, but the experience had to be put down, expressed somehow — nor would I like to have it misunderstood. Although I wrote it under the pressure of strong feelings, I did not intend it as a negative statement, nor do I think it is. On the contrary. However, the imagery must be carefully considered, perhaps prayed over.

The Oak
Raining.
Quiet
And gray.

An oak
Stripped
Of summer
Glory
Stands
Naked
On the horizon
Of my thought;
Branches
Reach to the sky,
Pleading
For spring.

Was it only yesterday
I walked
Among the sick,
And silent
Laid my hand
On flesh
Cool to the touch,
Skin
Stretched taut—
A mask
Moving
In pain,
Eyes lidded
In deep-circled wells
Of acceptance?

Life,
So joyous
And secure—
A candle flame
Gasping
For air!

Wasted woman!
Winter
Shall wrap
Your awkward branches
For an eternity.

Ave!
Ave
Mar-
i-
a—
You loved
And carried a man
Within you,

As woman should —
But,
One more birth,
Darker yet to mind
Remains.
So, let us rejoice
And meet
At the birthing place
To wait
The first breath
Of dawn.
Then we shall walk
With our burden
Of love
To the fields
Of the dead —
Like a medieval woodcut,
In black
And white —

There
We shall bury
The aftermath!

Again the image of the tree, this time shorn of its leaves, standing straight and firm, weathering all the storms, even the final one.

Suffering and prayer had become one in this woman, a remarkable person, one I couldn't get out of my mind. Her funeral was simple and elegant at the same time. And somehow everyone in that church — and it was filled — knew that her death had been for them.

If we could see the cause of our suffering and understand it in terms of what happens to us and others, it would cease to be suffering; but this also means that the good would cease to be.

To suffer — and this may sound strange — is to enter the shadows beneath the fig tree; getting away from the self for a while. I say it may sound strange. What I mean is this: the one who suffers is certainly *aware* of himself, but as undergoing something he would rather be free from, and in that sense he is involved in a highly selfless activity. It's true that suffering can harden a person, but more often it seems to soften him, opening him up to what is most fine in life. We are in the shadows, it is true; and that means we are cut off from the light.

A person cannot bear suffering and be entirely selfish.

In the darkness of suffering — and I'm not talking about a major disaster — old idols come crashing to the ground, idols that say we are independent, omnipotent, and have a right to "take" without giving. Our spirits are stretched as they begin to exercise themselves in coping with the unexpected and painful. Suffering can be the most intense prayer. And in the darkness, we see a new light — better, we see by another light not our own.

Suffering can make us honest by burning away the dross of everyday compromise with ourselves and with God. And if we are honest, we shall see the truth hidden beneath that dross. This holds true even for the suffering involved in disappointments. Have you ever had the experience of suddenly realizing that you had been following an illusion? When something happens to make you stand still and take a good look at yourself? And what follows as you compare your activity with what the Lord wants from you — perhaps what you were doing or thinking was no more than a carefully concealed deception. You were convinced of the goodness of your motives, that they were unselfish, and then you were made to look at your true motive. The result? Shock — and *real* suffering! You are disappointed in yourself, and that can be the keenest form of suffering, easily as sharp as physical pain only not visible (so there is little or no sympathy or compassion from others to soothe it). That kind of suffering must be turned into prayer. It must be put into context, related to something higher than yourself to have any meaning. To relate the suffering—seeing it as being potentially good, even—is to take the sting out of it. Prayer does that; or, rather, to relate your discovery to something higher is to pray.

It is also in the suffering that Christ can work by the power of his Spirit.

Suffering can be and often is a crisis. The original meaning of that word, *crisis*, is "a contest, struggle, or judgment in which something important is decided." Kairos time. Just as you can't rush kairos time, so you can't rush suffering and get it all over with in a hurry. But by relating it to someone and something higher, it becomes a force for good. That is the meaning of Saint Paul's thought in his letter to the Romans:

> We know that by turning everything to their good, God cooperates with all those who love him . . . .
>
> (Rom 8:28 JB)

I was fortunate enough to visit the leper colony made famous by Damien De Veuster, the priest who lived for sixteen years on that little finger of land devoting his life and death to caring for his "children." The leper colony sits at the base of a mountain 2,500 feet high, and is located on a thin strip of land only three by two and a half miles. On three sides it is surrounded by the ocean. There are still lepers living there—in fact, many of them do not want to live anywhere else! In the hospital the patients who are seriously ill with the disease are cared for by the sisters and doctors.

One day, about five years ago, I went through the hospital and made the acquaintance of about six of the patients. The first man I met was in a wheelchair. What I noticed was that a few of his fingers were missing and his skin was discolored. I talked with him for a while and he asked me for a blessing, which I gave him. Four years later, I visited the hospital again, and without knowing it, I was led into a room where this same man was, a room for the blind. He was in bed, one leg amputated, both eyes gone, his nose and the central part of his face decomposed. I had no idea whatever that this man was the same man I had met earlier. The priest showing me around, and introducing me to the patients, said to the man: "Here is a Jesuit father from the mainland to visit you; ask him for his blessing." The man sat up in bed and what he said to me showed that suffering and prayer had become one in him. There was no unhappiness in his voice, no sadness. Perhaps the best way to tell it is through a prayer-poem I wrote after leaving the colony — and after thinking a great deal about it:

> He wore
> An old T-shirt
> Stained
> Tobacco brown
> Beneath his arms;
> One eye
> Carved out,
> The empty socket
> Still pleading;
> The other — purple,
> Discolored, milk-green —
> Focused vaguely
> With sound.
> His flesh
> Hung slack
> In folds
> Of wallpaper

Paste gray.
And one leg only
Stirred
Beneath the blanket.
A fetid smell,
Mixed with medicine,
Filled the room —
Leper!
Lawyer, too
Standing in the courts
Earning attention
And respect,
Once.
   "Father!"
   The vague eye wanders,
   In faith.
   "Each night
   I rise at twelve
   And pray Christ's passion
   Till three."
And I wonder:
   "Why have I
   Two eyes
   And ten fingers?"

Then, Silence.

The empty socket
Still pleads,
And I see
For the first time
The cheap oleographs
Of Jesus, Mary
And Joseph, too,
Hanging
At the head
Of his tomb.

What incredible faith! Nor is this uncommon in the hospital that I visited on the island of Molokai.

God can turn even suffering into good. He can, in other words, draw good from evil, even the evil of emotional and mental sickness, and the far greater evil of

spiritual sickness. And that is the way in which the
following poem-prayer should be read, as the Lord drawing good out of evil. That is what I was trying to convey
when I wrote it. I was surprised at how deeply the evil
was entrenched and behind what subtle barriers!

The Prayer of the Self-Betrayed

O Lord
You are not content
With half a soul
Are you?
It's not enough
That you are acknowledged
Master,
Is it?
Every idol
Every false god
And contrary value
Must be purged
From the room
You occupy —
How painful your love is!
As it reaches
And challenges
The very images in my mind
That could act as a hiding place
For my embattled self!
And how disconcerting
To discover
They have no substance —
And in that discovery
Of self-betrayal,
I catch a glimpse
Of your purity
And love.

Peter could have prayed that prayer after he heard
the cock crow the third time, and after he rushed outside
and wept bitterly. In fact, he probably did pray

something similar. How else could you explain Peter's extreme sensitivity to the Lord's question: "Peter, do you love me?" This was after the Lord's resurrection by the side of the lake when he took Peter aside from the other disciples to have a talk. Peter was very upset that he asked him three times (once for each denial!), "Do you love me?" Of course he did. Christ was the best thing that ever happened to Peter. That is why it was so painful for Peter to have to face himself after his virile boast that the Lord could rely on him more than all the others, and after his betrayal in which he swore up and down that he never even heard the Man's name before. Can you imagine, following the tears of discovery, what a shock it was for Peter to look *into* Peter? And yet, he didn't grow cynical or hard. He prayed it out. How? By relating it to someone outside himself. And that someone drew good out of the evil, the good of Peter's lasting repentance.

There is an ancient story that Peter wept so much recalling that night that two permanent grooves were worn into his cheeks. I'm sure they were tears of joy — not sorrow. And Peter is shown in some medieval polychrome wooden statues as quite genial, softened from the tough, hard, uncompromising man he portrayed early in the gospel story.

This line was written by Peter:

> . . . unload all your worries on to him, since he is looking after you.

> (I Pt 5:7 JB)

Quite a switch in tone from the man who boasted in front of all the disciples that he, Peter, would never betray the Lord, not even if it meant the loss of his life! Suffering and love had done their work.

XI. THE RESULTS OF PRAYER

The River Rocks

How does prayer work its way into a person's life? Does anything happen that can be seen? My deep-down answer to that question is *yes*, but probably not by the person who is praying. It seems that others recognize a man of prayer. They see, and what they see would probably surprise the one who prays. There is a mystery here, and like all mysteries, it's impossible to dissect it, to get at its full meaning. But it can be grasped somehow, with respect and wonder. I remember one day going over to my brother's house to see him and his family. He had a new hobby and was telling me all about it. He took me out to the garage and showed me a small barrel-like machine driven by a pulley and motor. It was hardly bigger than a man's fist. He turned it on to show me how it worked and explained that he was going to take some stones, put them into the barrel and add powders that would, with the turning of the machine, grind down the rocks. I thought the whole thing was too long a process for my taste but decided that it would be good to show interest so that my brother would be encouraged to continue with his hobby. After all, he had a good-sized family and worked hard. He needed a hobby! And he had it too.

As I visited him over the following months, he told me what stage his rock grinding was at. He was using carborundum powder number 16 or some such thing which didn't interest me in the least; but I feigned interest and said, "Oh, that's nice . . . uh-hum, and what will you do next?" One day after about three months, during which time the little barrel with the rocks and the carborundum powder was daily doing its work, I visited my brother and he held out a small box and said, "Take a look at these, will you?" I had no idea what was in the box, so I took it and opened it and I found myself staring with fascination at jewelry — beautiful stones with what seemed to be rich, lustrous glazes. I said: "Gee, these are beautiful! Where did you get them?" My brother smiled the secret smile of justifiable pride and said: "These are the rocks I was grinding for the past few months." What happened next took less time than it does to write. I immediately saw in my head all the rocks in all the rivers of the world — all those crude boulders you stub your toe on, or throw at dogs, or build walls with — only I saw them polished! Shining like the jewels they were beneath that gray coating that looked so uninviting. And I saw jewels in the gardens, lining the lawns, under the water. Just imagine for one second what I was experiencing.

What had seemed uninviting and even dull had been transformed into a jewel. It was there all the time and I didn't know anything about it. And so it is with those people who pray. They are being polished, ground down until their brilliance shines out. It's a long and sure process, and God is the One who is polishing the stones. Prayer cuts through the rough exterior — grinds it away, and eventually transforms the person. To look for an immediate effect would be silly in such a process. Had I stopped the machine after only a few weeks to see what the effect had been on the river stones, I would have seen little that interested me. In fact, I probably would have turned off the machine for lack of conviction!

The effects of prayer are best seen over a lifetime, and they are best seen by someone else!

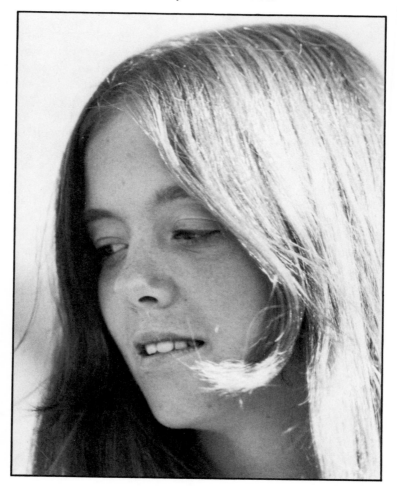